D1709417

OUTDOOR
SCIENCE
LAB

Life in the Soil

Lindsey Lowe

PowerKiDS
press.

Published in 2020 by
The Rosen Publishing Group, Inc.
29 East 21st Street, New York, NY 10010

For Brown Bear Books Ltd:
Text and editor: Lindsey Lowe
Children's Publisher: Anne O'Daly
Design Manager: Keith Davis
Picture Manager: Sophie Mortimer

Picture Credits
t=top, c=center, b=bottom, l=left, r=right
Interior: iStock: AlfFoto 14–15, Maren Winter 15b; Shutterstock: Aleh Alisevich 6br, anmbph
14br, Nikolay Antonov 1, 22–23, Elif Bayraktar 29tr, Maks Goncharuk 4, grafvision 23br, Aleksei
Gurko 4–5, Eric Isselée 23r, Kostasgr 27b, Piyawat Nandeenopparit 7br, NeutronStar8 6–7,
Emeline Ostmo 22br, Unal Ozmen 8–9t, photka 8–9tc, PPL 29br, RHJ Photo and Illustration 26b,
Mauro Rodrigues 29cr Manfred Ruckszio 8–9b, Snatia 28cr, schankz 5, Jon Shore 18br, Showcase
19b, Tomas Skopal 9, Anton Starikov 8–9c, StudioNewmarket 26–27, Takako Picture Lab 8br,
Rattiya Thongdumhyu 28bl, Bahadir Yenicer 29cl; U.S. Department of Agriculture: Agriculture
Research Service 18–19.

All other photos and artwork, Brown Bear Books.

Brown Bear Books has made every attempt to contact the copyright holder.
If anyone has any information about omissions please contact licensing@brownbearbooks.co.uk

Cataloging-in-Publication Data

Names: Lowe, Lindsey.
Title: Life in the soil / Lindsey Lowe.
Description: New York : PowerKids Press, 2020. | Series: Outdoor science lab | Includes glossary
and index.
Identifiers: ISBN 9781725314849 (pbk.) | ISBN 9781725314863 (library bound) | ISBN
9781725314856 (6 pack)
Subjects: LCSH: Soil ecology--Juvenile literature. | Soil formation--Juvenile literature. | Soils--
Composition--Juvenile literature.
Classification: LCC QH541.5.S6 L694 2020 | DDC 577.5'7--dc23

Manufactured in the United States of America

CPSIA Compliance Information: Batch-#BW20PK:
For further information contact Rosen Publishing, New York, New York at 1-800-237-9932

Words in the glossary appear in **bold** type the first time they are used in the text.

Contents

What Is Soil?............................ 4

How Is Soil Formed? 6

Kinds of Soil 8

🔍 Test Your Backyard Soil 10

🔍 Testing Soil Acidity..................... 12

Plants and Soil 14

🔍 Measuring Soil Content............16

Microscopic Soil Life 18

🔍 Making a Compost Pile 20

Worms and Snails 22

🔍 Making a Wormery.................... 24

Insects and Soil 26

Identifying Soil Creatures 28

Glossary 30

Further Resources......................... 31

Index 32

What Is Soil?

Soil is a natural substance that forms on the surface of land. It is important to all living things. There would be no animals or plants without soil.

Soil is a mixture of minerals, water, air, and **organic** material. There are many different types of soil, but they all contain these four basic substances.

↓ Soil is changed by farming. Plowing gradually breaks down the soil's natural structure.

↑ Numerous small creatures, including earthworms, live in soil.

Life Underground

Soil can be just a few inches thick or hundreds of feet deep. It contains tiny fragments or grains of rock. It also contains organic matter called **humus**. This is the **decaying** remains of dead plants and animals. Air and water fill any gaps between the solid materials in the soil. This mixture of air, water, and organic material is a good environment for plants, **bacteria**, fungi, and small animals. They live and grow in the soil.

↖ Soil may look solid, but it is full of spaces. Roots of plants reach down through the spaces for water.

How Is Soil Formed?

Soil usually takes tens of thousands, or even millions, of years to form. Sun, wind, and water break down rocks into tiny particles.

Soil begins to develop as a loose mixture of sand, silt, and clay. This mixture forms from small fragments of rock that are slowly broken down into even smaller pieces through a process called **erosion**. Organic materials rot and mix with the **inorganic** materials and water to form soil.

CLOSE UP

Crumbling Mountains

Mountain peaks look tough, but even the hardest rock is broken down by weather. When water freezes in cracks in the rock, it expands, shattering the rock. The sun's heat makes rock expand and split. Pieces of shattered rock form slopes of fragments, or scree. Over time, plants take hold in the scree and soil forms.

Soil forms from rock over many thousands of years. A slice down through the soil shows different layers.

It takes 500 years to produce just under 1 inch (2.5 cm) of topsoil!

Organic Layer

Topsoil

Subsoil

Parent Material

Bedrock

Soil Horizons

As soil matures, it develops layers. We call these layers **soil horizons**. Bedrock is solid rock. As it crumbles, it forms a thin layer over the bedrock. This is called the parent material. When water, air, living things, and decayed organic matter are added to the parent material, subsoil forms. This is soil rich in minerals washed down from the surface by water. The topsoil is rich in organic material and is the best quality soil for plants to take root. The organic layer (dead leaves and other organic matter) is at the surface.

When a plant dies, its roots mix with the parent material. Its shoots become part of the organic layer. This makes more soil. →

Kinds of Soil

There are many different kinds of soil. Minerals in the rocks, the climate, and the plants that grow in soil all affect its makeup.

Water and air give soil its texture. Clay and silt soils have fine, tightly packed **particles**. Water cannot drain away easily so these types of soil are usually very wet. The grains stick together in clumps, or clods. The stickiness of the soil makes it hard to dig. Sandy, gravelly soils have larger particles. They contain more air than fine soils. Water drains away quickly and the soil is often very dry. Loams are the best kinds of soil. They contain sand, silt, and humus. All kinds of plants grow well in loamy soils.

CLOSE UP

Soil from Volcanoes

Not all soil is formed from crumbling rock. Soils can form on the ash thrown out by volcanoes when they erupt. The minerals in the ash make good soil for plants. The plants root easily in the fine, crumbly soil.

These are the four basic soil types.

Loam

Sand

Clay

Silt

Acidic or Alkaline?

Soils also have different chemical makeups. Some soils are **acidic** because the rain that falls on them is acidic. Others are acidic because of the amount of rotting organic matter they contain. This produces carbon dioxide gas. When the gas dissolves in water, it makes an acid. **Alkaline** soil contains minerals such as sodium, calcium, and magnesium. It is less soluble than acidic soil. Alkaline soil is often found in deserts and other areas where it hardly ever rains.

Desert soils are dry. Plants grow in clumps and have long roots to reach water deep underground.

Test Your Backyard Soil

Aim: To find out what type of soil is in your backyard. Soil scientists describe the tiniest fragments of rock as clay or silt, the next biggest as sand, and the biggest as gravel. Each soil type has a different texture.

You Will Need

* A trowel
* A soil sample
* Seed trays
* Magnifying glass
* Tweezers
* Bowls
* A wide-mesh gardening sieve
* A fine-mesh sieve

1 Dig some soil from your backyard. Spread the sample out on a seed tray. Examine it with a magnifying glass and use tweezers to carefully remove any plants, insects, and other animal bodies. Put these in a bowl.

2 Tip the soil into a gardening sieve with a wide-mesh sieve. Shake it all through onto a seed tray. Pour the coarse material left in the sieve into another bowl, or tray.

When you have sieved your soil, take a small, pea-sized amount from each pile and squeeze it between your thumb and a finger. What can you feel? Make a note of your findings. If it is sandy, it will feel gritty. If it leaves a mark when you squeeze it, it will be silt or clay. Soil with a high level of organic material may feel spongy, and leak water when you squeeze it. Try testing other soil samples this way. Can you identify what type of soil it is just by feel?

3 Pour all the sieved soil into a fine-mesh sieve. Shake it all through. Pour the medium material left in the sieve into another bowl, or tray.

4 Sieving the soil in stages shows that every soil contains three grades of material, as well as living and dead matter. There is some fine material (silt and clay), some medium (sand), and some coarse (gravel).

Living and Dead Matter

Fine Material (silt and clay)

Medium Material (sand)

Coarse Material (gravel)

Testing Soil Acidity

Aim: Scientists describe the acidity of a soil in pH numbers from 0 to 14. The lower the pH number, the higher the acidity in the soil. A soil with pH 4 is very acidic, pH 7 is neutral, and pH 9 is alkaline. This project shows a simple way to test soil acidity.

You Will Need

* Red cabbage
* Saucepan
* Distilled water
* Measuring jug
* 4 glass jars
* 3 soil samples
* Labels
* Spoon

1 Ask an adult to chop up half a red cabbage. Put the cabbage in a saucepan. Add 2 pints (1 l) of distilled water. Ask an adult to boil the cabbage for five minutes, then leave to cool.

2 Strain the cabbage water into a jug. Pour some of the liquid into a small jar and put the jar to one side. This is the control sample to compare the other samples with.

Take a Note

The control sample in any science experiment is a sample that remains the same throughout the experiment. It sets the standard against which other results can be compared. In this experiment, the cabbage water is the standard. Try a similar experiment to see how plants grow in different soils. Plant a seedling in compost in a paper cup. Put the plant in a sunny position and water it daily. This is your control plant. Put different types of soil in three more cups. Add seedlings and water as before. Observe the plants. Which plants grow best, and in what type of soil?

3 Take small samples of soil from three different places. Make a note of where each sample came from. Spoon each soil sample into a separate jar. Label each jar so you know which soil sample it is.

Acidic (reddish)

Neutral (purple)

Alkaline (greenish)

Control (purple)

4 Half fill each jar with more red cabbage liquid. Shake the jars gently to mix the soil with the liquid, then leave to stand. With most soils, the color of the liquid will change quickly. A reddish color indicates that the soil sample is slightly acidic. A purple color nearly matching the color in your control jar indicates that the soil sample is neutral. A blue or greenish color indicates that the soil sample is alkaline.

Plants and Soil

Soil gives plants most of the water and foods they need to survive. But farmers use fertilizers to encourage plant growth.

Plants need some **nutrients** in large quantities. These include the gases oxygen, carbon dioxide, and nitrogen, and the minerals phosphorus, calcium, and potassium. Plants get oxygen and carbon dioxide from the air. Everything else comes from the soil. Minerals are dissolved in soil water and plants draw them up through their roots.

CLOSE UP

Plants and Nitrogen

Plants need nitrogen to make the proteins they need for healthy growth. A few plants, such as beans (right), get nitrogen directly from bacteria on their roots, but most plants get their nitrogen from the soil. Dead plants and animals release nitrogen, but not in a form that plants can use. Some bacteria "fix," or change, the nitrogen from the air in the soil into a substance that dissolves in water. This is then taken up by the plant roots.

Lettuce crops are sprayed with a fertilizer high in nitrogen for healthy leaf growth.

Fertilizers

Under natural conditions, plants use whatever nutrients are in the soil. But garden centers and farmers grow plants and food crops in large numbers. They need to add fertilizers to the soil to make up for the nutrients that have been used. There are two kinds of fertilizer: synthetic and organic. Synthetic fertilizers are usually made from chemicals. Organic fertilizers come from plants and animals, and include manure, compost, and ground-up bones.

Organic farmers fertilize their fields using animal manure and plant compost.

Measuring Soil Content

Aim: To measure the organic content of soil. Humus is brown organic material. It is formed from dead leaves and animal bodies that are broken down by soil **organisms**. It keeps the soil **fertile** and stops it from becoming too dry.

You Will Need

* Trowel
* Large soil samples from different places
* Several large, screw-top jars
* Measuring jug for water

1 Scoop soil from each sample into a separate jar. Fill each jar to the same level (about half full). You want to end up with roughly the same amount of soil in each jar.

2 Using the measuring jug, fill one jar about three-fourths full of water. Measure out and add the same amount of water to each of the other jars.

Keep a record of where you collected your soil samples. Label the jars. After a couple of days, what do you notice about your samples? Does one soil type contain more organic material than another? Can you use this information to identify which kinds of soil samples you used? Do you think the soil is loam, sand, clay, or gravel?

3 Screw the lids securely on the jars, then take them outside in case of leakage. Shake each jar vigorously for about 60 seconds to mix the soil with the water.

4 Leave the jars to stand. The mineral grains will slowly sink to the bottom of the jars, but the organic matter will float to the top. After a couple of days, compare the amount of floating material in each jar. This is the soil's organic content. Here, the sample on the right clearly has a much higher organic content than the sample on the left.

Microscopic Soil Life

Soil is swarming with life. Just two cups of soil can be home to 250 billion living things.

Many soil organisms are so small they can only be seen with a magnifying glass. These include creatures such as mites, springtails, and roundworms, or nematodes. Most soil organisms are even smaller. These include bacteria and fungi, which can only be seen with a microscope. They process nitrogen and minerals for plants to use.

CLOSE UP

Fungi

Fungi get their food by breaking down the tissues of plants and animals. They absorb juices from their **host** through thin threads called hyphae. Most fungi are microscopic. Only a few grow aboveground, like toadstools and mushrooms. Many fungi grow on or near plant roots, including many kinds of mycorrhizal fungi. Mycorrhizal means "fungus root." These fungi live in a two-way relationship with their host plant. They take sugar from the plant. In return, they help the plant take up phosphorus and nitrogen.

← Not all soil nematodes are helpful. The soybean cyst nematode lives in the roots of soybean plants. It kills millions of plants every year.

Living on Roots

A thin layer of soil called the rhizosphere clings to plant roots. Bacteria called rhizobia live in the rhizosphere. The plant gives them food, and the rhizobia give the plant nitrogen. The arrangement helps the bacteria and the plant. This type of relationship is called a mutualism.

The rhizosphere is a large area, as plants have lots of root fibers. →

19

Making a Compost Pile

Aim: To make a compost pile for study. Compost is a mixture of soil and decaying organic material. Farmers and gardeners use compost to improve the quality of soil. It gives it extra nitrogen and helps it to drain better.

You Will Need

* Brown material, such as dead leaves, dried plants, pine needles, and newspaper torn into small bits
* Plant sprayer
* Green material such as grass clippings, green plants, and cabbage leaves torn into small bits
* Handful of soil
* Trowel
* Tank

1 Put a layer of brown material in the base of the tank. Brown material is rich in carbon. A glass tank is used here to show you what is happening. If you have a backyard, you can make a compost pile later by digging a pit about 18 inches (45 cm) deep, or you can use a well-ventilated bin or box.

2 Make sure the brown material is torn into small pieces and spray the layer thoroughly with water. This speeds up the process of decay.

3 Next, add a layer of green material. It should be fresh, recently living bits of plants and vegetable scraps. Green material is high in nitrogen, which is good for the health of soil and plants.

4 Spray the green layer with water. Continue to build up alternate layers of brown and green material, spraying each layer as you go. Add a handful of good soil. This contains **microorganisms** that will help start the decay process. The process of decay makes the pile warm inside. Turn the compost over with a trowel every few weeks to keep it well aired. Spray it with water if the weather is dry. In about a month, the brown and green stuff will have turned into crumbly brown compost.

Worms and Snails

Bacteria and other microscopic life are not the only organisms in the soil. There are visible organisms, too.

Soil is a rich habitat for small creatures called invertebrates. These are animals without a backbone. They include worms, slugs, snails, centipedes, and many different kinds of insects. Some invertebrates are protected by hard shells. Others are soft, like worms.

CLOSE UP

Garden Snails

There are more than 80,000 kinds of snails. They live on land, in freshwater, or in salt water. Land snails, such as garden snails, live in soil in damp, shady places. They eat plants, which helps to recycle plant matter. This helps to make compost and soils. They also eat some kinds of soils that contain calcium. This makes their shells strong.

About half a million worms live in 1 acre (0.4 ha) of soil.

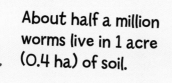

Earthworms

Earthworms help to keep the soil healthy so that plants can grow. As they burrow through the soil, they loosen it, which increases the amount of air and water held in the soil. Worms also break down organic matter into food that plants can use. Worms eat their way through the soil, swallowing any material in their path. They break down the dead matter in the soil and push it out of their bodies as a trail called a casting. This leaves behind a rich natural fertilizer.

Slugs live in damp soil or rotting leaves and plant matter. When the weather is very dry, they dig deep down into the soil.

Making a Wormery

Aim: To make a wormery so you can study the behavior of worms close up. This project uses compost worms, not garden earthworms. You can use the compost they make in your backyard.

You Will Need

* An old fish tank
* Damp newspaper
* Damp compost
* Half a dozen compost worms from a garden supplier
* Fruit and vegetable scraps
* A cloth for covering the tank

1 Line the bottom of the tank with a sheet of damp newspaper. Then scoop in some damp, good-quality compost and a few damp, scrunched-up balls of newspaper.

2 Sprinkle the compost with water, then gently put the worms on the compost. If you don't want to touch the worms, ask an adult to do it for you.

Take a Note

Watch the tank over a few months and take notes. Observe the worms' burrowing habits. How long does it take for them to make castings? Note how long it takes for the scraps to disappear and the level of compost to rise.

You may also notice the number of worms increasing. After about six months you will have too many worms. Empty half the mix into the yard. Every couple of months, scoop off the top layer of compost and add it to the soil in your backyard.

3 Feed the worms by scattering small pieces of fruit and vegetables on the surface. Do not feed them oil, fat, or meat. They don't like orange or lemon peel, or onion or garlic, either.

4 Add a sprinkling of water, then cover the tank with a layer of cloth and tape it firmly in place. Make plenty of air holes in the cloth using a skewer or needle. Put the tank in a cool, dark place and leave it for a few weeks.

Insects and Soil

Thousands of insects and bugs live in the soil. They eat plants and other animals. The waste they leave behind feeds the soil.

Insects are small animals with six legs and a hard outer shell called an exoskeleton. Most insects also have wings and antennae, or feelers. Ground beetles are hard and shiny. Some kinds of ground beetles live in burrows in the soil. They feed on creatures that live in topsoil, such as root maggots. Many beetles that live aboveground lay their eggs in soil. The grubs are the first, or larval, stage of a beetle's life. They live in the soil and eat the roots of grass and other plants.

CLOSE UP

Soil Organic Carbon

Like other animals, insects play a role in recycling carbon. Plants take in carbon dioxide from the air. They use the carbon dioxide to make food in a process called **photosynthesis**. Animals take in carbon when they eat plants. Dead animals, insects, and plants decay in the soil and release carbon. This is called soil organic carbon, which is released into the air.

June beetles bury 50 to 100 eggs in the soil. After about three years feeding on plant roots in the soil, adult beetles appear.

Ants and Termites

Ants and termites build their nests underground. They burrow tunnels and chambers through the soil. This helps to loosen the soil and spread organic material. Some ants eat dead plant matter. Others are **scavengers** and feed on whatever they can find. They take food back to their nests, where uneaten food rots and feeds the soil.

Ants and termites dig their nests underground. They leave a telltale mound of soil above the ground.

Identifying Soil Creatures

How many of these creatures have you seen in your backyard or under the microscope? Can you identify them from the descriptions below?

Mammals

The largest soil animals are burrowing mammals, such as gophers, moles, and badgers.

- Warm blood, fur, four legs, two eyes

Mole

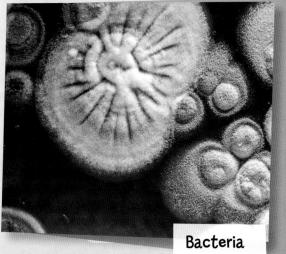
Bacteria

Bacteria

Bacteria are the most numerous of all soil creatures. Bacteria include rhizobium and actinomycetes.

- Can only be seen through a microscope

Algae

Moist soil teems with algae, which are plantlike organisms that are too small to see with the naked eye.

- Algae contain the chemical **chlorophyll**

Green Algae

Fungi

Fungi often grow in the soil and feed on living, dead, or rotting matter.

- Most feed through threads called hyphae

Mushrooms

Arthropods

The easiest soil animals to see are **arthropods**. Insects are arthropods.

- A hard body case, three or more pairs of legs

Woodlice

Worms and Mollusks

Soil contains many creatures with soft, sausage-shaped bodies, such as worms. Worms and mollusks include earthworms, snails, and slugs.

- Long, soft bodies, some with shells

Earthworm

Glossary

acidic Describes a substance with a low pH that can taste bitter and eats away other materials.

alkaline Describes a substance with a high pH.

arthropods A large group of small creatures with a hard body case and many legs.

bacterium (plural **bacteria**) A single-celled microscopic organism.

chlorophyll The green chemical in plants that converts sunlight into energy.

decaying To break down or cause to break down slowly by natural processes.

erosion The wearing away of something by the action of wind, water, or other natural happenings.

fertile Capable of producing healthy plants, and food for microorganisms.

host An animal or plant that provides food and gives support to another organism living in or on it. The host does not benefit from the relationship.

humus The dark brown part of soil made from the decayed remains of plants and animals.

inorganic Something that does not consist of, or come from, a living thing.

microorganism A living thing so small it can only be seen with a microscope.

nutrients Proteins, vitamins, and minerals essential for life and growth.

organic Something that is made from, or comes from, living matter.

organism A living thing that has one or more cells.

particles Tiny bits of material.

photosynthesis The way leaves use the sun's energy to make sugar from air and water.

scavenger An animal that feeds on dead or decaying material.

soil horizon One of several layers in the soil.

Further Resources

Books

Graham, Ian. *You Wouldn't Want to Live Without Dirt!* New York, NY: Franklin Watts, 2016.

MacAulay, Kelley. *Why Do We Need Soil?* New York, NY: Crabtree Publishing, 2014.

Oxlade, Chris. *Soil.* North Mankato, MN: Capstone Press, 2016.

Sherman, Jill. *Fertile Land and Soil.* New York, NY: Enslow Publishing, 2018.

Websites

Dig Deeper
www.soils4kids.org
The Soil Society of America shares educational resources for students about soil, its role in our communities, career exploration, and experiments.

Easy Science for Kids
www.coolkidfacts.com/ germination-for-kids/
Information on soil, including video, quizzes, and fun facts.

The Food and Agriculture Organization of the United Nations
www.fao.org/world-soil-day/en/
Website celebrating World Soil Day, which is held in December every year.

Soil Science Society of America
www.soils.org/discover-soils/ soil-basics
A website describing what soil is, soil types worldwide, career advice, and much more.

Index

A
acidic 9, 12, 13, 30
acidity 12
air 4, 5, 7, 8, 14, 23, 25, 26, 30
alkaline 9, 12, 13, 30
ants 27
arthropods 29, 30

B C
bacteria 5, 14, 18, 22, 28, 30
beans 14
beetle 26, 27, 29
burrows 26
calcium 9, 14, 22
carbon 9, 14, 20, 26
carbon dioxide 9, 26
casting 23, 25
centipedes 22
chlorophyll 29, 30
clay 6, 8, 9, 10, 11, 17
clods 8

compost 13, 15, 20, 21, 22, 24, 25
crops 15, 19

D E F
deserts 9
earthworm 5, 23, 24, 25, 29
eggs 26, 27
exoskeleton 26
farming 4, 15, 20
fertile 16, 30
fertilizers 14, 15, 23
fungus 18

G H I
garbage 21
gardeners 20
gravel 8, 10, 11, 17
ground beetles 26
grubs 26
hermaphrodites 23
humus 5, 8, 16, 30
hyphae 18, 29
insects 5, 10, 22, 26, 27, 29
invertebrates 22

L M
loam 8, 9, 17
maggots 26
manure 15
microorganisms 21, 30
millipedes 29
minerals 4, 7, 8, 9, 14, 30
mites 18
mole 28
mollusks 29
mountains 6
mushrooms 18, 29
mutualism 19
mycorrhizal 18

N O P
nematode 18, 19
nitrogen 14, 15, 18, 19, 20, 21
nutrients 8, 14, 15
organic 5, 7, 9, 16, 17, 23
oxygen 14
parent material 7
phosphorus 14, 18
photosynthesis 26, 30
plowing 4
potassium 14
proteins 14, 30

R S
rhizobia 19
rhizosphere 19
rock 5, 6, 7, 8, 10
roots 5, 7, 9, 14, 18, 19, 26
sand 6, 7, 8, 9, 10, 11, 17, 26
scree 6
silt 6, 8, 9, 10, 11
slug 22, 23, 19
snail 22, 29
soil horizons 7, 30
springtails 18
subsoil 7
sugar 18

T V W
termites 27
topsoil 7, 26
volcano 8
water 4, 5, 6, 7, 8, 9, 11, 12, 13, 14, 16, 17, 20, 21, 22, 23, 24, 25
weather 6, 21, 23
woodlice 29